Lavonne J. Adams
~~Lavonne J. Adams~~

Through the Glorieta Pass

WINNER OF THE
2007 PEARL POETRY PRIZE
selected by DAVID HERNANDEZ

Pearl Editions
LONG BEACH, CALIFORNIA

Library of Congress Control Number: 2008934499

Copyright © 2009 by Lavonne J. Adams
All Rights Reserved
Printed in the United States of America

ISBN 978-1-888219-36-4

Book design by Marilyn Johnson

Cover illustration: Frederic Remington (American, 1861 – 1909),
　　　　　　　　Indians Simulating Buffalo, 1908, oil on canvas,
　　Toledo Museum of Art, Gift of Florence Scott Libbey, 1912.1

This publisher is a proud member of

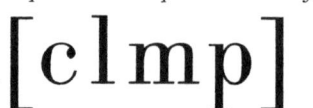

COUNCIL OF LITERARY MAGAZINES & PRESSES
www.clmp.org

PEARL EDITIONS
3030 E. Second Street
Long Beach, California 90803

www.pearlmag.com

THROUGH THE GLORIETA PASS

To Jon —
It has been such a pleasure to share our rainy time in VT. I will always remember Caspar's smile as the absent sun. Best of luck with your writing. May our paths cross again.
 Lavonne
(VSC, July 2009)

PEARL POETRY PRIZE SERIES

Fluid in Darkness, Frozen in Light • Robert Perchan
Ed Ochester, Judge, 1999

From Sweetness • Debra Marquart
Dorianne Laux, Judge, 2000

Trigger Finger • Micki Myers
Jim Daniels, Judge, 2001

How JFK Killed My Father • Richard M. Berlin
Lisa Glatt, Judge, 2002

Earth's Ends • Andrew Kaufman
Fred Voss, Judge, 2003

The Farmgirl Poems • Elizabeth Oakes
Donna Hilbert, Judge, 2004

This Big Fake World • Ada Limón
Frank X. Gaspar, Judge 2005

Denmark, Kangaroo, Orange • Kevin Griffith
Denise Duhamel, Judge 2006

*As always, for Micah, Miranda, and Veronica Volborth;
and for Laura Richards, whose spirit equals those of the women in this
collection.*

Acknowledgments

I would like to thank the following, in which poems appeared:

Asheville Poetry Review: "Murphy Wagons"
Missouri Review: "Marian Sloan"; "Julia Anna Archibald";
"How the Earth Became Bountiful"; "Apache."
North Carolina Arts Council: "NC Laureate Host Poet of the Week":
"Ernestine Huning"; "Yellow-Haired Woman, Cheyenne."
Red Rock Review: "Jicarilla Apache, Shaping Clay."

I would also like to thank the University of North Carolina Wilmington for the 2005 Summer Research Initiative Grant; the faculty, staff and students of the Creative Writing Department, University of North Carolina Wilmington, for ongoing encouragement and inspiration; Yvette Neisser Moreno, Sarah Messer, Daniel Terry, and Katie Kingston for thoughtful reading, advice and encouragement.

For additional assistance and support, Veronica Volborth; Jack McCausland; Michael Richards; Anthony Kellman and Robert Parham; the women of the Red Tent Book Club; Mark Gaskill; Steve Gehrke; Ele Byington; Michelle Manning; Marilyn Johnson. A special thanks to Marc Simmons for his impressive commitment to Santa Fe Trail scholarship. And finally, to Melissa Floyd, Steve Schnitzler and the folks at Port City Java, Market Street, for always making me feel welcome.

Contents

Foreword by David Hernandez ix
Introduction xi
Timeline xiii

How the Earth Became Bountiful (A Cheyenne Tale) 1
Susan Magoffin 3
How Humans Became Mortal 11
On the Far Side of Tucumcari Butte 14
Anna Maria Morris 15
Jicarilla Apache, Shaping Clay 21
Marian Sloan 22
Apache 26
Kate Kingsbury 28
Barter 33
Murphy Wagons 34
Marian Sloan, Return to Missouri 35
Sioux 38
Julia Anna Archibald 39
Comet 43
Wind Tamer 44
Ernestine Huning 45
Yellow-Haired Woman, Cheyenne 51
Photograph, After the Nun's Death 53
Sister Blandina 54
Notes 62
Bibliography 64

Foreword

I was immediately impressed with Lavonne J. Adams's *Through the Glorieta Pass*, and by immediately I mean the first line of the first poem: "Long ago, the Plains were a hollow bowl." Right away, Adams conjures up a desolate scene, the right metaphor for that emptiness, a rhythm that sways along with graceful musicality, a voice full of intelligence and insight, and the perfect line for the Great American Novel—all in only *ten* syllables. Clearly I was dealing with a gifted poet.

Through the Glorieta Pass is like no other collection I've read before. Conceptually, the book is a union of voices: Adams's straightforward and lyrical one, and the voices of women who braved the journey across the Santa Fe Trail. In poem after poem, Adams lets the dead speak to us— and their stories are harrowing. Deadly winter storms. Men crushed by wagons. A woman's breasts carved away by an Indian's knife. It's an apocalyptic view of the Old West where disease was rampant, the innocent were scalped, and buffalo carcasses rose from the landscape "like trail markers."

Although these stories originate from the journals of those who traveled the Trail, in the end these are Adams's poems, her enlightenments, and they shine from the page like gold sifted from a stream. She is a big-hearted poet of great eloquence who is sensitive to the sounds of each word. I refer to you a passage from "Murphy Wagons":

> The better drivers tuned their ears to the music
> of their wagon, to variations in the timbre
> of each creak and groan.

So here you have it: the music of Lavonne J. Adams's poems. She is one of our better drivers.

—David Hernandez
Long Beach, California
September, 2008

Introduction

During the mid-1800s, prior to the arrival of the Atchison, Topeka & Santa Fe Railroad, the Santa Fe Trail was the route used to open up the Southwest. Unlike the Oregon Trail, which existed in order to move settlers to the west, the Santa Fe Trail was primarily established for reasons of commerce. The Trail, which began in Independence, Missouri, covered approximately nine hundred miles and took up to three months to travel. The Trail itself splits into two branches—the Cimarron Cutoff, which ran southward through the desert, and the Mountain Branch, which wound through the treacherous Raton Pass in the Rocky Mountains—before reuniting at La Junta, New Mexico. Each branch was notorious for its particular tribulations. The title of this collection refers to the final pass through the Sangre de Cristo Mountains, which leads into Santa Fe.

While some of the travelers were drawn to the adventure of the West, others took to the Trail for health reasons; the climate was said to be extremely beneficial, especially for those suffering from lung ailments. Many of the women who traveled the Trail did so in order to remain with husbands who relocated to Santa Fe for business reasons. They kept journals or wrote memoirs that relayed the trials, as well as the glory, of the Trail. These poems are very loosely based on those recollections. This collection is meant to open an alternative window into history. While I have endeavored to capture accurately the experiences these women endured, the final product is intended to be art—historical fiction rather than fact. The poems are punctuated by Native American folklore/myth, and laced with glimpses of the roles of both the Native American and Mexican women who made their homes along the Trail.

—*Lavonne J. Adams*

Timeline

1846: Susan Shelby Magoffin's journey; U.S. seizes New Mexico

1849: Abduction of Ann White from the Santa Fe Trail

1850: Wagon Mound Massacre; Anna Maria Morris's journey

1852: Marian Sloan's first trip on the Santa Fe Trail

1854: Kate Kingsbury's journey

1856: Marian Sloan's return to Missouri

1858: Julia Anna Archibald Holmes's trip West; appearance of comet

1859: Launch of the Windwagon

1860: Marian Sloan's second trip to Santa Fe

1861: Civil War begins

1863: Ernestine Huning's journey

1867: Massacre of the Huning in-laws

1869: Battle of Ehyophsta (Yellow-Haired Woman) with the Shoshone

1872: Sister Blandina travels to Trinidad, Colorado

1876: Sister Blandina instructed to go to Santa Fe

1880: Railroad first arrives in Santa Fe, effectively making the Trail obsolete

1881: Construction of the Loretto Chapel's winding staircase

How the Earth Became Bountiful
(A Cheyenne Tale)

Long ago, the Plains were a hollow bowl.
Babies too hungry to cry hung in their cradleboards
from bare trees. When they could no longer bear
empty cooking pots and hollow eyes, two warriors
set out to search for whatever they could find.
After seven days, a butte rose in the distance
like a buffalo's back. An old woman
stepped through the waterfall
as if it was the flap of her tipi. Her skin was
as brittle and lined as cornhusks, her hair
as white as an antelope's belly. Above her
cooking fire hung strips of dried buffalo meat.
Why have you not come sooner, my grandsons?
She handed the warriors two bowls filled
with stew, two bowls filled with corn.
While they ate, she pulled porcupine quills from
a buffalo-bladder pouch, softened
each quill in her mouth, flattened them
between her gums. With an awl
and sinew, she stitched the quills to a pouch
shaped like a turtle, which would hold
the earth's umbilical cord—a guarantee of its longevity.
The bowls were still full when the warriors could eat
no more, their stomachs firm as fish.
The cowry shells sewn to the woman's bodice glowed
like the moon's sisters as she lifted her arm, pointed
to her left. In a haze of sage smoke, the warriors saw
the earth laden in buffalo. Behind the woman,
fields bristling with corn; to her right,

prairies thick with horses. Straight ahead,
they saw their own faces fierce as they fought
alongside their tribe. And they knew this was
an omen—that they would be victorious,
that they would carry home many captives,
and that the storm clouds forming in the east were
nothing but shadows.

Susan Magoffin

I.

On the trail, I witnessed such beauty. Pressed
between the pages of my journal, wildflowers

I gathered as I walked alongside the wagons, my favorite
with leaves that felt like fur—at the end of its stalk,

clusters of yellow flowers brushed with brown, each
shaped like its own small hourglass. I tried not to think of

the snakes with mosaic backs, instead
I focused on the green bug collared in gold

that looked like a shrunken alligator. It sauntered
across the hot rocks, posed with one leg lifted.

When it turned in my direction,
there was something human

in the way it raised its head—
like a bald old man listening

for a memory.

II.

The bank of Ash Creek was steep,
but smooth, the creek bed dry.
Over and over I see the sky tilting,
the rocks rising to meet me,
the shrill cry of the mules,
the crack of our carriage shattering.
As we fell, *mi alma* cradled me
in his arms, kept me
from being crushed. At the end
of the month, when we reached
Bent's Fort, I delivered
blood and what would have been
a son. *Come unto me*
when your burden is heavy
and I will lift it. Later,
I was told that at the same time,
within the fort, an Indian woman
birthed a lusty son. Half an hour later,
she bundled him to the river where
she bathed them both—cold water
against tender skin, her rough hand
holding his head like a chalice.

III.

Only three weeks out,
one of our Mexicans died
of consumption. Eight men

dug a grave deep enough
to keep wolves at bay.
I'm accustomed to the cruelty

of death during childbirth,
of men maimed at work,
of floods and storms and

the omnipresent threat of disease—
diphtheria, cholera, consumption.
I've always trusted in the compassionate

mercy of our Lord. But here
on the trail, the corpse was rolled
in a blanket, covered with stones,

with dirt. What comfort
for his family? That night,
the stock were corralled over his grave

to tamp it down. Beneath
a blank moon, the sound of their lowing
an approximation of grief.

IV.

> "It created sad thoughts when I found myself riding almost
> heedlessly over the work of these once mighty people."

When we passed Pawnee rock, I climbed
to the sandstone facing, soft enough
to carve my name with a well-honed knife.
How long until wind and rain will
wear those letters away?
                                  From a distance,
Pecos Pueblo looks like a beehive, abandoned
and crumbling. The only sound is the rustle of grass.
Montezuma promised to return to his people
as long as the fire he kindled was not allowed to die.
But all that's left is the scent of ash.

At the far end of the ridge, the remains of a mission—
the Franciscans' quarters little more than a maze.
Where the church stood—a door, an altar,
a few dark beams supporting patches of ceiling.

V.

I often danced the cotillion at home:
rugs rolled up, floor beeswaxed to a mirror,
camellias blooming on the far side of the sill.
Silk gloves and perfect manners.
In Santa Fe, the fandango is presented
as if it were a play—two dancers saunter
to the center of the room, the woman dressed
in row after row of black lace, her skirt
so short her ankles are exposed.
Her castanets snap a heartbeat,
her partner claps his response.
The guitar thrums faster and faster,
halting when the dancers freeze, their passion
mimed by the pulse at the base of their throats.
While their bodies never touch,
their gaze never wavers. *Mi alma's*
fingers brush the back of my hand.
I blush. In a corner,
a señora with a necklace heavy as a yoke
lights a cigaritta, rests her feet
on a kneeling servant's back.

VI.

There are times when I gaze at
my dear husband's face and fear
my devotion to him surpasses my love
for our Heavenly Father. Is it possible
to love one without slighting the other,
too easy to turn from the unseen
to what can be touched?

When Governor Bent's home was swarmed
by a mob of Pueblos drunk on
the whiskey we sold them, he refused
to raise his weapon, fearing harm
to those most dear—his wife and his children
who were huddled at his side. His caution
bought time. His neighbors tunneled through
the wall between his house and theirs,
spirited his family away while the mob dug
through the ceiling as if the governor was ore
they were trying to mine. They took
his scalp, nailed it to a board, paraded it
through town like a hide stretched to dry.

VII.

I taught these Mexican women
a better way to knit—in return
I have learned how tortillas are made.
First, soak dried corn until
the husk peels easily away.
Place a handful or two of this grain
on a grinding stone, hollowed
in the center from years of use.
With a second stone, grind
the corn to paste.
Your arms will ache
from the stone's weight.
Grease the sheet of iron
that rests on the fire like a griddle.
Cook and turn. Repeat.
This is my version of water into wine—
dried corn transformed into
something steamy, almost sweet.

VIII.

In that strange Eden, I napped on buffalo robes.
The wagons, with their five-foot wheels and
billowing canvas, were whales rising

from the sea, waiting to swallow some Jonah.
In the worst storms, water streamed
across the tent's floor, transforming

our bed into its own sweet ark. At times,
I feel that journeying down the Trail
was a way of living my religion—

each mile reshaped me, though
unlike Lot's wife, I shall refuse
to look back.

How Humans Became Mortal

At first,
the woman thought the words her child babbled
were a miracle, that like the medicine man,
he was able to speak the tongue of the Great Spirit.
But his tongue thickened until he couldn't swallow,
his eyelids fluttered like a wounded bird,
his arms became hollow reeds. Others moved
their tipis away.
               How had her family earned
the buffalo spirit's ire?
                      Alone, her husband
now casts his buffalo stone, waiting for an answer
the way he usually waits for portents
of good hunting. He remembers
the last buffalo rock he rode past
rising like an omen above the prairie's grass,
and how he had offered the buffalo spirit a scrap
of pemmican rather than the perfect eagle
feather he had found the day before.
He hunkers outside the tipi, rubbing grease into
the arc of his buffalo stone—no larger than a knuckle—
as if his care can undo what has been
happening to his son.
                   The woman dreams
a herd of buffalo dances around her tipi,
their soft grunts cadenced like music,
and she knows the dream is a sign
to search for the Father of Buffalo.
In the morning, two magpies cross and re-cross
the rising sun as if stitching it to the sky.

She follows them until the sun sets
behind a buffalo skull altar where He guards
a hole in the earth that sometimes hides the buffalo.
He looks older than the prairie, the bones
of his back humped with years of power.
Why are you here?
                    When she describes her son's
sickness, he nods his head. *Look around you.*
My buffalo calves die in the jaws of wolves and bears,
are singed by prairie fires, fall through spring ice
where cold water steals their lungs.
Why should you humans be different?
                          She doesn't know
how to respond, lowers her head, fearful
beneath his unwavering gaze. But somewhere
in his heart is a piñon nut of pity. He leads her to
the creek behind his tipi, points to a spot
where a rock and a buffalo chip nuzzle
against the bank. *Choose. If the one you pick floats,*
your son will be spared. If you choose
wrongly, at their appointed time,
every human will drop to earth the way
your choice will drop to the bottom of the creek.

She fears this is a puzzle she cannot solve.
Her hands feel weighty, her palms are
slick with sweat. She thinks about how,
when she grinds a chip to powder, it sifts
between her fingers, drifts in the breeze.
Common sense turns her eyes in the direction of the chip.

But then her ears begin to ring, and she remembers
the story of how her husband discovered his buffalo stone,
how he heard it singing from the grass, and
she tells herself that this rock is singing
its buffalo song to her. She lifts her hand.

The thunder of her mistake shudders
through her body as the rock disappears, leaving
nothing reflected in the creek's calm surface
but the vast blue sky, cool and inscrutable.

On the Far Side of Tucumcari Butte

For ten days, the dragoons and their scout,
Kit Carson, tracked a band of Jicarillas
who abducted Ann White somewhere

along the Santa Fe Trail. For ten days they came
across pieces of her clothing—a dusty shoe, a dirty bonnet,
the ragged flounce of a petticoat—in what remained

of makeshift camps. They refused to halt their pursuit
though each morning the Jicarillas split into groups,
their tracks scattering like buckshot.

The desert was a monotony of sage and hardscrabble.
In the distance, Tucumcari Butte was stoic, shined
with neither love nor hate, neither blessing nor curse.

When the dragoons finally arrived within gunshot range,
Carson urged a charge, but the captain chose
to parley, a tactic that allowed the Indians to flee.

Fluttering in the clutter of what was left behind,
the pages of *Kit Carson, Prince of the Gold Hunters*.
How many nights had Ann White read this novel

as if it were the Bible, how many nights dreamed
of an encounter with its hero, whose life had become
a blanket spun from less than a bucket of truth?

She must have run toward her messiah-in-buckskin.

Her body was still warm when he found her;
her hand curled into the dust, the shaft of an arrow
rising like a sapling from her back.

Anna Maria Morris

I.

For six days, it has rained.
There is little to do but huddle
here on the bank of Big Turkey Creek,
water twelve feet deep and rising.
The soldiers have cleaned their guns
and cleaned them again, hunkered
on the bank as if they were soothsayers
able to predict the weather by
whatever the water churns up.
There is no wood for our fires,
very little grass; the livestock are restless.
Panting but well-pleased, the Mexican
we hired returns from a four mile excursion
with a packet of wood bundled on his back.
I pour him a glass of brandy,
hand it to him as if I was Prometheus
and this liquid was a gift smuggled
from the hearth of a distracted god.

II.

This past month, I grew accustomed
to the undulating grass of the Plains.
But what's now in front of me looks
like desolation. Desert. Even
the word tastes dry. Beneath

the wagons' wheels, rocks crunch
like cinders. Mottled sienna and brown, they are
pocked like worm-eaten wood, in places as glossy
as if coated in wax. Nearly weightless,
there is no real heft to this type of ground.
What is now Round Mound once was a volcano
that blistered earth's skin; dormant,
it looks like a callus chafed by the sun.

I was raised where landscapes had boundaries,
a certain circumscribed vision. But I knew
what it meant to marry a soldier, how discontent
can be like bread that refuses to rise—tasteless
and thick, impossible to digest. Our first night
on the trail, I drank champagne, served drinks over ice.
Now, senses alert, I anticipate even a glimmer
of water—the most turbid pond
as welcome as a prodigal son.

III.

Found at the Massacre Sites—
    A boot torn across the heel;
    the hammer from a gun;
    a mailbag's strap;
    a scrap of canvas with an unidentifiable stain;
    eight arrowheads;
    small chunks of charred wood;
    bolts scattered like acorns;
    a collar, a sleeve;
    a copper coin stamped *The free state of Chihuahua,*
        a quarter bearing the image of an Indian
        clutching his bow and arrow;
    the bent barrel of a rifle;
    tatters of paper,
        some with numbers, others with shreds
        of faded conversations;
    a well-formed skull with beautiful teeth

IV.

A brutal winter storm.
On the downswing of the Trail,
the oxen of a man named Brown
dropped to their knees, air frozen
deep inside their chests.
When the wind died, he was left
with only a few mules
and his wagons—a ghost town
of creaking wood. For a hundred
bitter mornings he scanned the horizon
for some sign of rescue. Indians
found him first. Before
they could take his life, in a gesture
of resignation or despair, he gifted
the only squaw who met his gaze
with his rare white mule, earning
her pleas on his behalf.

Now, I see the same white mule
in the distance, like a rising moon.
On its back is the squaw who—
in the past year—has become legend
for saving Brown's life.
Her skin is the color of steeped tea,
her clothing is clean and neat;
I didn't expect such strength
in the cast of her shoulders,
in her imperturbable gaze.
A chief's wife, she wears her own
authority as if it were a robe, weighty

with beading and quills. She gestures
toward my diamond ring, offers
the brass bracelet from her arm.
I shake my head no. As she walks away,
I watch the fringe of her skirt
and feel something close to regret.
How long would that metal have held
her body's heat? How long
would I have felt its warmth
seep into my wrist?

V.

One private drowned in a swollen river,
some wagons were lost, and we were stalked
by cholera, yet our trip along the Trail wasn't
considered excessively grueling. The soldiers were
rarely short on rations and their duties were
clearly defined. Is not some measure of comfort
found in knowing what to expect? At least

once a week the cooks roasted a ration
of coffee beans over smoldering coals, tied
the coffee and a broken egg inside a square of
cloth. The packet was dropped into a pot
of boiling water. After four minutes,
a generous splash of cold water
was tossed in to settle the grounds.

Our first glimpse of Santa Fe—a town
built of clay—was the dash of cold
water that settled the grounds
of our hopes. Two days after we arrived,
an artillery soldier said he was weary
with life, put his gun to his head. Why,
I wondered, when we had finally reached sanctuary?
Could it be possible that what tries us
most sorely is what we need to survive?

Jicarilla Apache, Shaping Clay

This is a sacred place where
the earth shelters the richness of clay
the way a woman protects her womb.
Run the clay through your fingers, winnowing
fragments of bone, small rocks, stray roots.
For purity, relieve yourself in the bushes
before you begin. For balance, divide
your hair in two, tie each section
on the side of your head. For sanctity,
refrain from mating until the final
pot is set aside to dry. Earth, air,
fire, water—you are an extension
of what is sacred. If you must speak,
whisper, or your noise will enter
the pot and cause it to shatter.
Let your wet fingers work the clay,
slick as afterbirth, until it is eggshell thin,
until it is more than the promise
of what can be held.

Marian Sloan

I.

When we left Fort Leavenworth, smoke
from tar barrels smudged the sky,
the lining of my nose—a talisman
against cholera. On the trail,
gray ribbons of smoke rose
from each campfire as
tents became Japanese lanterns lit
by the lamps inside. Twice a day
I gathered buffalo chips in my skirt
like a windfall of apples. I learned
to kick each chip with the toe of my shoe,
to expose what was hidden in its scant shade—
red spiders that uncurled to the size of
my hand; scorpions that scurried away,
their tails curled like dark questions.

II.

At Fort Marcy, walls crumbled, wind
and rain eroded the soldiers' graves, stranding
bones to bleach in the sun. We piled them up
like firewood, then—as one child counted to fifty—
the rest of us ran to hide. One by one,
we sneaked back, free only when a bone was snatched
from the stack. What did we know
of respect for the dead?

Late one afternoon, I walked past the jail.
Through the door's bars, I watched
a prisoner pull a cigarette from his pocket.
He smiled and asked my name, then told me his
daughter had braids as long as mine.
To make me smile, he sang
Shoo-fly, don't bother me, then swung
his silver pocket watch as if it was that fly.

The next morning I carried him two cookies
that smelled like molasses and ginger.
There was a red stain on his shirt. His head
was lowered as if deep in prayer.
At his feet, the cigarette, still unlit.

III.

Once a month, when the Indian Scouts paid
my mother for their room and board,
we went to Spiegelberg's store for supplies,
its dirt floor still damp from water sprinkled
to keep the dust down. In a glass case,
a display of candy—fat licorice babies,
cinnamon drops as hot as the red chiles
that hung like witches fingers outside the door.

But it was rock candy I craved, the mysterious
way the crystals clung to the wick, each sharp edge
and odd angle a terrain my tongue longed to explore.
With the handle of a knife, I could break off one
piece at a time, tuck it under my tongue
like a sweet secret. Sometimes
the crystals were faintly cloudy,
sometimes they seemed almost amber,
as if trying to transform into gold.

IV.

I made myself a pouch—like an Indian's
medicine bag—from a Bull Durham tobacco sack.
Inside, three gray horsehairs wound around
a chicken feather, a moss agate, a nugget
that glittered when tipped toward light.
When I tied the bag around my waist, I became

invincible. My mother's heart was
her medicine bag. Inside, she bundled the spirits
of her husbands—one, an Army surgeon killed
in the Mexican War; the other, a scout ambushed
by Indians. How often did their restlessness
snag like tumbleweeds inside her veins.

On the trail, livestock were corralled at night,
loosely bound so they could graze at will. Still,
by morning several found their way out,
as if the stars were salt licks waiting
for their dissatisfied tongues.

Apache

My belly is a spring river, swollen.
Soon, this child will come.
I have done all that I should—eaten
no liver to darken the child's skin,
turned away from the plump berries
that would leave their own pink marks.
I don't want this little one to enter
the world standing, so refuse
to eat any animal's feet. And I no longer
look at Slow Walker, with his foot like a club,
or at my husband's grandmother,
with her eye turned white as snow.
When I offered my sister's small daughter
both bow and burden strap, she reached for
the burden strap—as if the bow was little
more than windfall kindling—and I knew
it was a daughter kicking my heart.
For seven days, I have worked this
buffalo skin, pegged it to ground, scraped away
what tissue remained. I have soaked
the skin in water and ash until
the calf's golden hair became a paste
I could wipe away. When the skin is
soft as cattail-down, I will shape it
into a small tipi for my daughter's play,
that she may learn early
the ways of women—how to boil
buffalo's horns in water to shape them
into spoons; to mix meat and fat,

pound it into pemmican. How to
gain our people's respect by sharing
whatever wealth she has. Each morning,
as I grind corn, I glance up at the sky,
where the clouds couple and break apart,
and I know her name will be Clouds Moving,
that she will have a spirit like the white buffalo,
rumored yet rarely seen.

Kate Kingsbury

I.

I knew what to expect,
had watched my neighbor die
from consumption, had burned
the final bloody towels. By the time
I was twelve, I recognized flushed cheeks
and eyes bright as a bird's
for what they were. Now, I feel
the scorch of my own breath,
my chest a tinderbox brimming with coals.
Men travel west to test their mettle,
to escape the burden of proper manners,
to better their finances through trade.
But others like me long only for
dry air that will not fester in lungs,
our desire to live like a match flaring.

II.

In cool months, oysters were
worked from the blue-black bottom

of the Chesapeake Bay, iced
inside oaken barrels, sprinkled

with a blanket of cornmeal. We carried them
with us on the long journey west.

As the ice melted, the cornmeal drifted
down like golden plankton, nourishing

the thriving oysters. A touch of steam,
the blade of a knife, pressure at the crevice

where two halves of shell clasped—
the oyster was pried open. Inside,

a memento of what had been left behind—
a pouch of salty sea glistening like a mute tongue.

III.

My friend Lillie birthed her son one month before
I birthed mine. The larger her body became,
the more she was sickened by the smell
of tortillas grilling. At night she dreamed
of loaves of bread, crusty and full,
that she would tear open like a ravenous wolf,
its yeasty steam a tunnel to carry her home.

It has been a year since tears mingled on our cheeks.

Now, here in Santa Fe, even the sky seems
farther away. I imagine Lillie strolling
through her New England forests laden with snow.
Above her, wind blusters through the treetops,
shaking free the last of each bough's cold burden.
Sycamore, pine, maple, elm: my mouth shapes each word
over and over, as if they were an incantation,
as if they were a prayer.

IV.

Wind swept away what remained
of the brief bitter winter
and the sky lightened to tin. Yet
I heard no chirping from my canary—
it lay at the bottom of its cage
like a premonition. That day
and the next, I refused to eat, closed
the curtains over every window, shut
the door to the few I called friend,
sat with my son Georgie on my lap.
He was born fragile, his bones
forged by my disease, his palate twisted
into its own soft beak. When he first nursed,
milk ran from his nose in thin, sweet trickles.
I was afraid he wouldn't survive. But
hope is like a dream of flying—beautiful
until you open your eyes.

V.

I'd forgotten how this Massachusetts air settles
like damp rocks in my chest. I cough

as if I'll never stop. Am I too sick to travel,
am I too sick to stay? Some nights

I awaken drenched in my own sweat,
my gown like wet laundry. On warm afternoons,

I walk Salem's streets as if pacing the perimeter
of my own waning life. In the weeks before

Georgie died, at the base of his nails
faint blue moons rose, the color of the crocus

I later watched unfurl from his grave.
I will birth no other children to leave behind.

But somewhere, in the distance, Santa Fe
calls to me, rises like the New Jerusalem.

Barter

Before the last tortilla is fried and packed,
the mutton and goat meat dried;

before the punche tobacco is plugged
and corn-husk rolling papers soaked and trimmed;

before the final *coton* is woven, buttoned
across a loved one's chest like supple armor;

before the wagons are choked with
thousands of pounds of wool;

when sticks are sharpened into cattle-goads
and gourds for water are hollowed,

each Mexican wife barters with God or
Fate through the effigy of her favorite saint.

She shrouds it in cloth and tucks it in a hand-hewn chest
as if it were a coffin, as if the saint could take her husband's place.

She knows what it means for him to work on the trail—
each day, eighteen hours of running alongside the wagons,

fed only two tortillas and two onions like small twin globes,
like wheels tumbling down his parched and bitter throat.

Murphy Wagons

> "I want to know what you are doing on this road.
> You scare all the buffalo away." —Sitting Bull

Consider the weight of what was carried:
7,000 pounds of blankets, suspenders, boots,
gin, whiskey, rum, raisins, sardines,
dirks, pistols, chisels, hatchets.
Yet even a wagon can be a work of art.
Joseph Murphy gauged his wagons' aged
wood by the feel of its grain, searching
for what was most durable. Only saplings
were lathed into spokes, their moist wood
more resilient. Instead of wielding an auger,
he burned every hole a size smaller than the bolts—
charred wood was less likely to rot, each joint
was more snug. Consider how, in the dry air,
wagons rumbled themselves apart—axles snapping,
wheels splitting, spokes dropping out like rotten teeth.
The better drivers tuned their ears to the music
of their wagon, to variations in the timbre
of each creak and groan. They soaked wheels to swell
wood; tightened loosening tires with wedges;
splinted wagons minus a wheel with a pole
that trailed eight feet behind, like a stick dragged
through dirt by a bored child.

Marian Sloan, Return to Missouri

I.

Diamond Creek's pools were thick with tadpoles, a lush feast
for hungry rattlers. A few feet away,
on the far side of a sod wall, children gathered
to toss dirt clods until dust rose like smoke.

We were thrilled by our own temerity,
by the angry rattles that peppered the sky,
by what we had heard:
>   if you pull out a rattlesnake's fangs,
>   new ones will grow like slivers of venomous moon;
>   if you don't die from a snakebite,
>   at the same time every year you'd writhe
>   on the ground as your skin mottles like a snake's belly.

Deep in the sod wall, another rattler stirred.
The arrow of its head inched from a crevice—
its tongue flicked forward, tasting
the calico of my favorite blue dress.

II.

A cabin. Inside, two trappers—scalped.
Food on the table, still warm. And somewhere
out there, John Brown and the Border Ruffians
who are said to murder women and torture children
with glee. Against such odds, our caravan

of twenty wagons were deemed not enough, so
the men decided to remain at Diamond Springs
until another train came into sight or
the military swept through like a flash flood.
But after two weeks, my mother decided
to walk our way to Council Grove.

I wanted to wait in camp
with my brother and our wagon,
with the few children who were
part of the train, with the men
who refused to budge. But we left

under the final glimmers of moon.
The trail was furrowed,
as if every wagon was a plow.
I missed the crack of the bullwhips
and the moaning of the wagons,
our walk silent except for the rustle of our skirts
and the sound of our breathing. By midday,

the muscles in my calves burned
and my feet felt like sacks of grain.
We supped where honeysuckle grew

in tendrils down a stream's bank,
in an abandoned water wheel's shade.
I slipped into a nap. My mother's
gaze never strayed from the horizon.

Sioux

By the evening fire, we retell the story
of the warrior who caught his woman
with a rival, killed him, carved
a piece of meat from his back, carried it
still steaming in the early spring frost to
where his woman was soaking dried buffalo
for their stew. For a deed such as hers,
other women lose only the tip of their nose,
but he made her cook that meat and eat
before slicing her throat. Sobbing,
he dragged her body away.
                                        I can understand
the storm that drove that warrior.
When they brought my husband's body to me,
I heard the cries of a wild animal rise in my throat.
As if my knife had its own spirit, it gashed
my arms, my thighs—hot rivers of red pain
which I had to staunch with ash.
There were no arrows lodged in his body—
only small red moons surrounded by clouds of blood.

Much time has passed. Now, my mourning is over,
I am free to wash away the ash, to choose someone new.
Instead, I will prepare a feast for the other honorable women
who have lived with only one man. We will tell the stories
of our lives as if they were legends. Then,
I will bite the knife and vow to remain faithful
to my lost love, until I hear in the distance
the soft rustle of grass beneath my husband's moccasins
as his spirit travels toward me, coming to lead me home.

Julia Anna Archibald

I.

Since joining this train, I have worn
bloomers beneath a calico dress
that barely covers my knees.
I have become stronger, can walk ten miles a day,
have offered to stand watch at my husband's side.
Yet these men prefer I languish inside
my hot wagon, its flaps tied shut
against dust and any curious eyes.
Let me tell you what I've learned:
always cross a stream before camping—
by morning what was once tranquil
may become a raging river. Last week
my husband was offered two squaws
in trade for me. One Arrapahoe
with skin as burnished as copper, signaled me
to jump on the back of his horse. Even
as I shook my head no, I imagined myself
galloping across the plain,
the feathers at the end of his scalplock
like a wing against my cheek,
the pony's spine hard between my thighs.

II.

Buffalo move like gods across the plain.
Yet there is something like sadness
in the hump of their shoulders, in the weight
of their broad heavy heads. Something
like wisdom trailing from their bearded chins.
In gunny sacks, we carry their chips to use for fuel
when wood is scarce, cook our food over that fire,
supplement our diet with their meat. At Bent's Fort,
a Buffalo robe is worth ten cups of sugar.
Let me tell you about this calf. Only
a week old, it was too young to keep up
with the herd startled into stampede by our hunters.
Three times its mother returned to urge it along,
offering her life in exchange. To keep it alive,
the men bring it to me, as if my instincts were enough.

III.

Across the Plains, the Indians settle
their dead on stilts, the bodies drying
high above ravening wolves.
From a distance they look like altars
for an unknown god. How frail,
in comparison, the small white crosses
at the base of Wagon Mound,
where ten massacred men
were consigned to ground.

Many Christmases ago, I pierced
oranges with so many whole cloves
that I could barely see a sliver of peel.
On wide red ribbon, I hung them
in windows and in wardrobes
where they spiced our clothes with
their scent. Now, in a cruel parody,
I imagine the bodies of those men pierced
with arrows. Still, it's not those
ghosts that trudge through my dreams,
but the Apache princess captured and carried
to the Mound by soldiers who demanded
she point them toward her tribe. Instead,
in courage or desperation, she grabbed
a butcher knife and sliced deep into a mule's neck
before she was stopped by a soldier's bullet.

When I was young, I liked to stare at
the sun, its image scorching my eyes
so that for just a few seconds, I could see

its ghost wherever I looked—in patches of dirt,
hovering above the palm of my hand.
As we pass Wagon Mound, I imagine
the scorch of her spirit forever
burned into the horizon: arms raised, defiant.

Comet

> "The comet has been very brilliant for the
> last two evenings; it stretches clear across
> the Western sky." —David Kellog

Too soon to be the return
of Halley's comet, its head was brilliant
white, its tail first blue, then yellow—
like the dream of some ornate bird
streaking the night sky.

The natives predicted a hard winter. Death
would stalk the white man the way
white wolves stalk buffalo, snapping
at a hind leg until the hamstrung beast tumbles.

Yet how can anyone predict the slow waltz of heaven,
let alone the frantic tap dance of fate?

The Kiowas shrugged their shoulders, pulled
their blankets closer as the soldiers doled out
lumps of sugar. Brief, sweet puddles in their mouths.

Wind Tamer

What began as a Conestoga
became a Windwagon meant
to sail the prairie—the goal
to reach goldfields in six quick days.
Above the wagon's stacked cargo,
over the arc of its canvas cover,
another platform like a deck
where a crew of five could raise
their sails. They waited for
steady wind, envisioned
themselves disappearing
like a gull against the horizon.
Unfurling sails snapped,
puffed out like proud men's chests.
But energy harnessed
needs some form of release.
This wagon had no keel—
couldn't maneuver. Lines
pulled taut and stressed
planks groaned; each
wheel anchored into ground
too thick to cut. Outside Council Grove,
this innovation overturned like
misguided ambition, its twenty-foot mast
slamming to the ground
where the sails became a pale pond,
a cloth mirage rippling in the noonday sun.

Ernestine Huning

I.

I traveled under a lucky star, expected much
worse than buffalo carcasses like trail markers,
than the five wagons abandoned—like cast-off shoes—
after an Indian raid. Near Casa Depollo spring,
I gathered wild gooseberries—clusters
of pearls guarded by thorns long as needles.
Each day we made a feast of eggs and biscuits,
of ham and beans seasoned by our hunger.

I have heard travel is worse on the Oregon Trail:
exhausted men fall asleep, roll off their wagon's tongue,
are crushed beneath the wheels. Each family
packs a shroud and, for a coffin, clean boards.
Axles break, wheels shatter—to lighten the load,
what isn't needed is cast aside: clothing lying
in the dirt like orphans.
                      I brought with me
a table and chairs, canned truffles
and a brass cage shaped like a corset
that holds ten canaries I refused to leave behind,
each a flurry of gold I can hold in my hand.

II.

> *"It is a queer feeling to experience a storm out on the open prairie."*

Near dusk, a storm swept across the prairie.
The clouds were cliffs casting shadows
like dark continents. I felt each clap of thunder
in my heels, as if I were perched on
the skin of a drum. The sky seemed
heavier than land—I couldn't imagine that
anything could keep them apart, or
that there would still be enough air for me
to breathe. Everything I valued
seemed insignificant—
my china plates, my husband's eyes,
my own throbbing body.
Lightning cast the sky asunder.

III.

On the way to Santa Fe, our cook stared
at the lines in my palm, fingered each
rise and drift in my skull, told me my fortune.
She promised a large house full
of furniture polished smooth as a lake,
a porch wide enough for a dozen children,
a sky so blue it would make my eyes ache.
Yet how could she not hear the future
echo of my brother's screams?
How could she not see where an Indian's knife
would carve away my mother's breasts,
how feathers from her bed would stick
to each wound, how the hair of her scalp
would swing from a belt like the pelt
of some animal? Or my husband
as he galloped away, the taste of fear
like blood pooling in his mouth?

IV.

My husband's first letter said only that
they had been attacked, that brother Fritz
was wounded. My mother, he added,
had been weakening on the trail.
Her heart. He feared she wouldn't make it
through the day. The next letter said
she had passed away peacefully,
and that my brother had followed,
an infection from the wound curdling
his blood. But the truth is
like cream that churns to the top.
I learned that the Cheyennes
were on the warpath, after an entire village
of tipis had been burned. Still,
it was not my husband's fault
that he couldn't find a larger train to join,
or that my mother would find the field
of sunflowers that unrolled like a quilt
before them so pleasing. The barouche
could travel faster than the other five wagons,
so they ended up too far ahead.
And it was certainly not his fault
that the soldiers from Fort Zarrah
were escorting their women on an excursion
to pick wild plums twelve miles away.
It was not my husband's fault
that he rode the only mule. Later,
he confessed that instinct
made him dig his heels into the mule's side

when the Indians war-whooped toward him,
that he turned back toward the fort, raced
seven miles for help. Some would say
this was common sense. Some would say
that shame and regret wear the same
scuffed boots.

V.

The Spanish women always dress
in black, one year's mourning
for a loved one lapping a year's
mourning for the next. I find my comfort
in a house scrubbed clean, in a border of lilacs
along the path. Life will always be a balance
between what happens and
                    what could have happened.

Every day at four, I serve the servants
wine and cake. When I ring the bell
that calls them in, the mass
of blackbirds smothering the cottonwood
rises, circles like a cyclone,
then settles back on the branches,
squawking like a harsher mistress.

Yellow-Haired Woman, Cheyenne

Look at these arms. They throw spears,
wield knives, shoot bows. Why should I
be bound to camp waiting for the warriors'
return, to be satisfied with waving scalps
from the end of poles around the fire.
Is it enough to pray to the Great Spirit
for my husband the first four mornings
he is gone—each time I pull a pot of meat from the fire—
as if these muttered words could make him invisible
to enemy eyes? You have heard the stories of
what I have done. When the Shoshones sneaked
like coyotes into our camp, thinking we were weak,
I ran my knife between many ribs. How is killing
an enemy different from gutting a buffalo?
When we found their final warrior cowering
in the cleft of nearby rocks, it was not I
who wanted to question him—my only
question came from my knife as it sliced
beneath his arm, as I carved away his scalp.

Let me tell you a secret. In the society of women
who fight beside men, we have our own
red-stone pipe carved like a magpie's beak.
The bowl is female, the stem is male—
there is power only when they are joined.
Like the men, we fill the pipe with kinnikinnik,
light it with a buffalo chip, then pass it
from hand to hand, each of us lifting the pipe
toward the sky, the earth, the four sacred directions.

We understand truth, we know the strength of ceremony.
We are not women who will mourn for those lost in battle
by gashing our foreheads, by wandering the brush alone.
Instead we plan war parties, pound the pemmican and
sew sturdy moccasins, ride behind our warriors,
our war cries rising until they're clutched in
the Great Bird's claws, returned to the Earth as thunder.

Photograph, After the Nun's Death

The wind lifts the wimples of two nuns kneeling
by the grave, and the shawls and coat tails

of those who are walking away. Frozen forever
in sepia, one nun buries her face in a handkerchief,

the other covers her eyes with her hand. Grief
is etched in the angles of their bodies,

in the submissive slump of their shoulders.
Consider how difficult it was to nurse

the cholera-ravaged nun through her final
struggle—the humbling bouts of diarrhea,

every muscle knotting, her pulse
trickling away, her pleas for water

she couldn't swallow. Imagine
this photo as a tableau vivant,

that you can suddenly see the restless
horse sidling, hear the muffled

sobs of the nuns, the murmuring
of the others as they turn back

toward their lives. Within minutes,
the frame will be empty except for a solitary

rattler curled beneath a clump of sagebrush.
By morning, only the simple cross

will cast its scant shadow.

Sister Blandina

I.

"No virtuous woman is safe near a cowboy."

Before I left Cincinnati,
I was warned
about cowboys, that the dark
bonnet and white collar of
our order are little deterrent
to those who don't know
their meaning.
I traveled the first day alone.
Clean hay filled the bottom of
the stage, smelled like autumn's
shadow. Then there he was—
tall, lanky, a buffalo robe draped
like a scapular over his shoulder.
His broad-brimmed hat hid his eyes;
his gun was a gargoyle curled
against his hip. Outside,
the driver cracked his whip;
slowly, the wheels began to turn.

II.

These men raise cocks to fight: a maelstrom of dust,
blood, and feathers. The following day
the victor is buried to its head like some odd squawking flower.

From a half-mile away, the men begin to gallop—
the object, to scoop up the bird by its head and
carry it away like a trophy. There is no mercy.

On Good Friday, I watched *penitentes* mimicking
our Savior's pilgrimage to Calvary—they thrashed
their blood-pocked backs with strips of cactus.

A few days later, two settlers were murdered. The same
penitentes formed a posse, searched until they found
what they were looking for—four Mexicans, belligerent

in their refusal to confess to a crime they didn't commit.
But the compass of suspicion always points Native. With less regret
than for a horse gone lame, they were hung

from the nearest tree, bodies slung into a wagon then
dumped like slag in an abandoned hut. I'm accustomed to
laws laid out like bricks in a wall, but in Trinidad,

men grab what they can—a piece of stolen land stolen again.
The few caught and locked away tunnel like termites
through adobe walls, escape before the circuit judge can unpack his gavel.

Even the town's leaders practice chicanery—two schemed
to cause a mine to collapse, to claim what remained
as their own. They realigned wooden supports so the slightest touch

would send the ceiling tumbling, a waterfall of rocks and dirt.
Confrontation is useless. Subtlety is a language I've had to learn.
I sent for a former student, an Indian I knew I could trust,

persuaded him to get hired, to enter the mouth of the mine
before the sun lightened the sky, to point out anything suspicious,
to search for gunpowder and hidden fuses as if they were veins of gold.

III.

Thirty-five orphans, seventy-two patients,
sixteen sisters to feed and the vegetable garden
looked like the aftermath of a plague of locusts.
Should I rely on faith or my own ingenuity?
The cook held an empty pot as if begging for alms.
At the back of our plot of land, an adobe wall
marked the archbishop's garden, where vegetables were
buried heads-down, their roots like Eve's hair drying
in the sun. After an easy leap, the skirt of my habit
became a cornucopia of what was not mine—
parsnips, onions, cabbages. But beneath each
leaf, a worm of shame gnawed on grains
of self-righteousness. By the time I knocked
on the archbishop's door, I was covered
in dirt, as if my actions had bound me
closer to earth. "I have come to make a confession
out of the confessional." But he urged me
to take what I needed. The following morning,
more was delivered from his larder—
sacks of sugar and coffee as heavy as my pride,
its brew a scorching sacrament against my humbled tongue.

IV.

I never expected death, yet it was always there,
like a moon moving through its phases. Once,
I nursed an Irishman, McCaferty, who had been shot
in the leg with buckshot. For a week the tin leaked
its poison into each muscle and sinew—
the law of cause and effect made manifest,
the way the nature of sin breeds the seeds of
redemption.
                    Years ago, the Chief of the Utes declared
his son dead, yet when a wagon bearing "the corpse" arrived,
I discovered he was still alive. To these Indians,
a man is dead when he has no heart,
when the pulse becomes a frail bird tapping
inside a wrist, when the spirit is an eagle
already flown.
                    Mr. O'Leary died
from an illness I didn't know how to fight.
He wouldn't eat, barely slept. Each day
his spirit folded more tightly upon itself.
I ran from his body after the doctors splayed it open
as if something had been lost inside, but made myself return
to face the fear of what each of us will one day become—
a mound of cooling clay, no longer malleable.

V.

Adjacent to the cathedral, the unfinished Chapel
of the Sisters of Loretto remains
a test of patience. M. Mouly, the first architect
who returned to France stone-blind
passed the project like an heirloom to his son,
who was later shot by a jealous husband.
As if anguish were its own dark fuel,
the husband locked himself away,
pacing relentlessly, refusing
all sustenance. But compassion,
like the Stations of the Cross,
can be learned. After two bleak weeks
his wife returned home, shut their door
to the town's whirring tongues. Later,
this couple adopted a French orphan—
smallpox-scarred and blind in one eye—
as if her ruined face was a manifestation of
their flaws, as if her laughter could become
manna for their starving hearts.

VI.

Though the original design envisioned
a hallway that would link the choir loft
to the convent school, when the Loretto chapel

was deemed complete, the loft
was inaccessible, the chapel too small
to add a staircase. A covey of carpenters convened

but couldn't find a way to alter what had been
done, so the sisters directed prayers to St. Joseph.
On their novena's ninth and final day, a man appeared,

his tools packed on the back of a donkey.
He refused nails, soaked strange wood in vats
then pegged the pieces together, never speaking

beyond the language of his hands.
When his work was done, he disappeared
as if the horizon had plucked him up.

The staircase twists like a corkscrew, like a spit curl.
Thirty-three steps—no center support, no railing—
unfurl like a fan beneath my feet. With each step

the wood sighs as if it aches to tumble
back into planks. But I fix my gaze
on the rose window's mullions glimmering

above me like a vision, its blue so rich
it seems to seep into my skin. Ascension
is always an act of faith. I know that

I will not stumble; I know that I will not fall.

Notes

Susan Magoffin: A Kentucky bride at age eighteen, Magoffin is known as the first lady of the Santa Fe Trail (though there is evidence that others traveled the Trail before her). Susan Magoffin was married to trader Samuel Magoffin, and was the sister-in-law of James Magoffin, instrumental in the bloodless succession of New Mexico to the United States.

Pg. 4. *Mi alma* is a term of endearment that Susan Magoffin uses for her husband, trader Samuel Magoffin. Loosely translates "my soulmate."

"Susan Magoffin, IV." The italicized quote is pulled from her journal.

Pg. 7, Cigaritta: a term used by Magoffin in her journal.

Anna Maria Morris was married to Major Gouverneur Morris, the commanding officer of the 3rd Infantry. Both came from very wealthy and prestigious New Jersey families. She was thirty-six years old at the time of her journey.

"How Humans Became Mortal": This poem is very loosely based on one of the "Foolish People" tales of the Apaches. These tales were meant to be instructional, illustrations of the things that a smart Apache would never do. I was, however, intrigued by what may have actually inspired the foolish woman to choose a rock over a buffalo chip. Pemmican: a mixture of dried buffalo meat and fat. Buffalo chips: the dried excrement of the buffalo.

Marian Sloan (later Marian Sloan Russell): Traveled the Santa Fe Trail numerous times, the first at age seven. After the death of her father, then of her step-father, Marian's mother planned to relocate to California, where Marian's grandfather was mining for gold. When he and both of his sons died of cholera, Mrs. Sloan signed on as a cook with the famous Santa Fe Trail wagon-master Francis Xavier Aubry. The family made the trip back to Missouri in 1856, but then returned to Santa Fe in 1860.

Kate Kingsbury: Though she was already ill with consumption (tuberculosis), she married trader John Kingsbury, her brother's business partner, in December 1853. While her son George was born deformed (January 1855), the true nature of these deformities is not known. After visiting her family in New England, Kate Kingsbury died of her illness on 5 June 1857, at the Lower Arkansas River Crossing, while on the return trip to Santa Fe.

"Barter." Based on the recollections of José Librado Gurule, as told to Mrs. Lou Sage Batchen in 1940. Punche tobacco is a blend of tobacco and a wild plant that was cut and dried. It was used to roll cigarettes. *Cotons* are hand-woven coats, cut to the waist in front, longer in the back.

Julia Anna Archibald (Holmes): Known as one of the early "bloomer girls," Ms. Archibald wore a dress to her knees with pants beneath. Though married, she referred to herself by her maiden name with the exception of when she signed letters to her mother.

"Wind Tamer." My thanks to Todd and Ilana.

Ernestine Franke Huning: Married to trader Franz Huning, who emigrated from Germany in 1849 at age 22. In St. Louis, on his way home after a visit to Germany in 1863, he met and married Ernestine, who was also of German descent.

"Ernestine Huning, III." The italicized quote is from her journal, May 7.

Pg. 48, Barouche: a carriage with a collapsible top, two double seats that face each other, and an outside box seat for the driver.

La Glorieta was the name of the Huning's first home in Albuquerque, New Mexico. The family home, Castle Huning, was built in 1883.

"Yellow-Haired Woman." Her Cheyenne name is Ehyophsta.

Pg. 51, Kinnikinnik: the tobacco mixed with spices that was smoked by the Indians.

"Photograph, After the Nun's Death." The photograph, taken in 1867, is from the archives of the Sisters of Charity of Cincinnati, Ohio. The three nuns were the first Sisters of Loretto sent to Santa Fe.

"Sister Blandina, I." The italicized quote was advice given by Mr. Tart and Mr. McCann upon Sister Blandina's departure for Trinidad, Colorado.

"Sister Blandina, II." The real culprits, Americans, were discovered two days later.

"Sister Blandina, IV." The incident with the Chief of the Utes occurred in Trinidad, Colorado, in September 1873. McCaferty died in the same location in November 1874. The death of Mr. O'Leary took place in Santa Fe in August 1879.

Bibliography

Arnold, Sam'l P. *Eating Up the Santa Fe Trail*. Niwot, Colo.: University Press of Colorado, 1990.

Barsness, Larry. *Heads, Hides and Horns: The Compleat Buffalo Book*. Fort Worth, Tex.: Texas Christian University Press, 1985.

The Buffalo Hunters. Alexandria, Va.: Time-Life Books, 1993.

Dary, David. *The Santa Fe Trail: Its History, Legends and Lore*. New York: Penguin, 2002.

Dunlay, Tom. *Kit Carson and the Indians*. Lincoln, Nebr.: University of Nebraska Press, 2000.

Gardner, Mark L. *The Mexican Road: Trade, Travel, and Confrontation on the Santa Fe Trail*. Manhattan, Kans.: Sunflower University Press, 1989.

Holmes, Kenneth L. *Covered Wagon Women: Diaries and Letters from the Western Trails, 1850*. Lincoln, Nebr.: University of Nebraska Press, 1983.

_____. *Covered Wagon Women: Diaries and Letters from the Western Trails, 1854–1860*. Lincoln, Nebr.: University of Nebraska Press, 1987.

Huning, Franz. *Trader on the Santa Fe Trail: Memoirs of Franz Huning*. Albuquerque: University of New Mexico in collaboration with Calvin Horn Publishers, 1973.

Lafarge, Oliver. *A Pictorial History of the American Indian*. New York: Crown, 1956.

Magoffin, Susan Shelby. *Down the Santa Fe Trail and into Mexico: The Diary of Susan Shelby Magoffin 1846–1847*. Ed. Stella M. Drum. New Haven, Conn.: Yale University Press, 1926.

Meyer, Marian. *Mary Donoho: New First Lady of the Santa Fe Trail*. Santa Fe: Ancient City Press, 1991.

National Geographic Society. *Trails West*. Washington, D.C.: Special Publications Division, 1979.

Niethammer, Carolyn. *Daughters of the Earth: Lives and Legends of American Indian Women*. New York: Touchstone, 1977.

Russell, Marian Sloan. *Land of Enchantment: Memoirs of Marian Russell Along the Santa Fe Trail*. Albuquerque: University of New Mexico Press, 1981.

Segale, Blandina. *At the End of the Santa Fe Trail*. Albuquerque: University of New Mexico Press, 1999. Reprint of the 1932 edition, originally published by The Columbian Press, Columbus, Ohio.

Simmons, Marc. *Murder on the Santa Fe Trail: An International Incident, 1843*. El Paso: University of Texas Press, 1987.

Simmons, Marc, ed. *On the Santa Fe Trail*. Lawrence, Kans.: University Press of Kansas, 1986.

Yenne, Bill, and Susan Garratt. *North American Indians*. Greenwich, Conn.: Brompton, 1984.

LAVONNE J. ADAMS grew up in Norfolk, Virginia, but has made North Carolina her home for the past thirty years. She is the recipient of the Persephone Poetry Prize for her chapbook *Everyday Still Life*, and the Randall Jarrell/Harperprints Chapbook Award for *In the Shadow of the Mountain*. She has published in over fifty additional venues, including *The Southern Poetry Review*, *Missouri Review*, and *Poet Lore*. She was an artist-in-residence at the Harwood Museum of Art, Taos, New Mexico, and has been awarded a Helene Wurlitzer Foundation Residency for Summer 2009. Adams teaches in the Department of Creative Writing at the University of North Carolina Wilmington.